Sarah and Paul Go Back to School

*Discover about the
Bible and about God*

Derek Prime

Christian Focus Publications

illustrations
by
Janis Mennie

Published by

Christian Focus Publications Ltd.

Tain   Houston
Ross-shire   Texas

© 1989   Derek Prime

ISBN 1 871676 18 5

CONTENTS

To Anna, Emily, Deborah and Andrew

1 The end of the vacation

Paul and Sarah MacDonald were twins. They were eager to start school again. Although they often pretended they didn't enjoy school, in fact they liked it very much. They were both excited about moving up a class. They'd heard a lot about their new teacher, and everyone who had been in her class before liked her.

'Are you glad you're going back to school, Sarah?' asked Paul.

'I think so,' said Sarah. 'It will be fun to go up, won't it?'

'Yes,' answered Paul. 'Miss Simon said that Mrs Fox's class is a very good class to be in.'

'I know,' said Sarah. 'She's supposed to be great at story-telling and she can draw very well. She makes her class draw plants and things, and the drawings are hung all round the walls.'

The weekend before they returned to school was an exciting one for Paul and Sarah, because it was their birthday on the Saturday. They had a lovely birthday party.

And they were given lots of presents - games to share, books and new sweat-shirts. Paul had a new football and Sarah a painting-by -numbers set. Both their Sunday School teachers had given them new hardback Bibles.

After the party Mrs MacDonald said, 'Why don't you go and collect together all your presents? You could tidy your bedrooms as well.'

'Oh no,' groaned Paul. 'We're always having to tidy our bedrooms! It's such a nuisance.'

'Oh yes!' replied Mrs MacDonald. 'Now you just do as you're told! Once you've tidied up you can enjoy playing with some of your presents.'

'All right,' said Paul and Sarah, with more of a smile on their faces now.

Once they'd finished, Paul went out into the garden with his new football. He enjoyed kicking it up against the wall, and then seeing how hard he could kick it as it bounced back to him. Sarah started her painting-by-numbers kit and was surprised how quickly time went.

****

On Sunday afternoon they were looking through the books they had received as birthday presents. Sarah had an exciting book about Mary Slessor, who worked in Africa as a missionary. Paul had a book about a doctor and his hospital in the jungle.

Paul turned over the pages of his book and looked at the photographs and drawings. As he read about some of the pictures he was very surprised. The book showed how people in some parts of the world did not worship the same God as he did. The pictures showed people bowing down in front of their idols made of wood and stone, which they called 'gods'. They all looked rather strange and ugly to Paul.

'Don't these people worship strange gods!' exclaimed Paul. 'Imagine carving a god out of a block of wood, or chipping one out of a lump of stone! It must take a long time to make them. But how silly to worship something you've made yourself. It's as stupid as worshipping one of those plastic models I've made.'

Paul rather enjoyed model-making. The hobby had all started when his father had bought him a model electric locomotive and

track for Christmas. He had enjoyed making the houses and shops and crossings so much that when he had finished them he went and bought some other plastic models to make, like Julius Caesar and George Washington. Julius Caesar had been rather a messy job because the glue hadn't set properly and had made the colours run. Now he thought of them as he asked his mother, 'Is there any difference really between these idols in my book and my models? Are these pictures of idols real gods?'

Sarah wanted to know the answer too. 'Why do they worship such idols, if they aren't real?'

Before Mrs MacDonald had a chance to answer either question, Paul added, 'I'm glad I don't worship strange things like that!'

'Yes, I'm glad too,' answered Mrs MacDonald quietly.

Paul suddenly remembered something else to ask his mother. 'Do you remember that missionary who came to church? He'd been with a tribe of Indians in Brazil. He told us he was the first outsider to go and learn their language because he wanted to write down the Bible for them. He showed us a photograph of a man who had been a witch-doctor. When he became a Christian he threw away all his idols and burned all the charms he'd used in trying to make sick people better.'

'Yes, I remember the missionary telling us that,' answered Mrs MacDonald. 'There's only one true God, no matter how many gods and idols people may worship. And the one true God is the Father of our Lord Jesus Christ. But, you see, we live in a country where most people have heard about the Lord Jesus. People can hear about Him in churches. We can read about Him, for we've the Bible in our own language. But there are lots of people in the world who've never heard about the one true God and His Son, the Lord Jesus. So some of them worship strange gods. They don't know the way to heaven.'

Sarah felt sorry for all the people who had never heard about the Lord Jesus, so she asked, 'Can't you get to heaven without knowing about the Lord Jesus?'

Mrs MacDonald replied, 'The Bible tells us that it's only through the Lord Jesus that anyone can go to heaven. Can you remember a hymn that says that?'

Sarah and Paul thought hard for a moment. Paul guessed it first. 'It's that hymn "There is a green hill far away". One of the verses says,

"*There was no other good enough*
To pay the price of sin;
He only could unlock the gate
Of heaven, and let us in."'

Sarah began to hum the tune immediately.

'The hymn's right,' explained Mrs MacDonald. 'Only the Lord Jesus could unlock the gate of heaven. He is the way for us to come to God. Men and women and boys and girls sin so much that they don't deserve to go to heaven. Indeed they deserve to be shut out.'

'It must be horrible to be shut out of heaven,' said Paul.'Last term when my class saw a film I was shut out of the hall as a punishment because I talked after Miss Simon told us to be quiet. I didn't like it at all.'

'It served you right,' Sarah told him. 'Three times Miss Simon told you to keep quiet!'

'No telling tales, Sarah,' interrupted Mrs

MacDonald. 'Just remember that it will be far worse for someone to be shut out of heaven. It will mean being shut out forever. But the Lord Jesus took the punishment which disobedient men and women, boys and girls, ought to suffer, when He died upon the cross.'

Sarah thought for a moment. 'The Muslim boy down the street doesn't believe in Jesus as we do. His family came from Pakistan. And then there's that Jewish girl whose father is a tailor. They don't believe that Jesus is their Messiah. Do they need to believe in the Lord Jesus too to go to heaven? God wouldn't want to shut them out of heaven, would He?'

'No, He doesn't want to do that,' answered Mrs MacDonald. 'That's the reason He sent the Lord Jesus to be our Saviour. God wants us to put our trust in the Lord Jesus as our Saviour. When we do, He's able to forgive our sins and to make us His children.'

Sarah looked at her mother and thought for a moment. 'But how do you know that what you say is right? Couldn't their gods be true gods?'

'That's a big question to answer,' said Mrs MacDonald. 'But the Bible, which is God's Word, tells us that these things are so. You'll find the answer to nearly all your questions in the Bible.'

'I'm glad we were given new Bibles for our birthday,' said Sarah.

'My old one was falling to pieces,' added Paul.

Mrs MacDonald smiled. 'Well, look after them, and - more important still - read them! Now who would like a doughnut and a glass of milk?'

2 Back to school

When Paul and Sarah awoke on Monday morning, the first day of the new school year, they were quite excited about going back to school; but they felt a little nervous at the same time. They had that strange feeling in their tummies - something like when they had to go to the dentist!

Mrs MacDonald could see that they weren't too happy about going back to school, but she didn't say anything to them about it.

But as soon as they arrived in the playground they felt much better. It wasn't long before the bell rang and it was time for school to begin. As they went through the doors the school seemed to smell especially clean, as if lots of people had been scrubbing the floors and polishing the furniture.

Paul and Sarah went into their new classroom, together with most of their friends, and met their new teacher. They were given desks at opposite sides of the room. It was fun having new desks, and their classroom had been decorated during the vacation.

Everything was fresh and clean. And everyone seemed well behaved that first morning of school - there was scarcely a whisper.

Mrs Fox spent most of the morning making her new lists of names, and giving out books.

'I want you each to write your name neatly and carefully on your notebooks, please,' she told the class. 'Your best hand-writing, don't forget. Now, while I finish all the jobs I have to do, please write on the outside of one of your notebooks the name of the subject as well - "English". Then write me a story called "My Vacation". Tell me what you enjoyed most while school was closed.'

Although Paul and Sarah sat at different sides of the classroom, they both wrote about their birthday party. Paul also wrote about all his presents, including the Bible from his Sunday School teacher. One of his best school friends called Philip looked over his shoulder and read what Paul had written. 'Fancy writing about getting a Bible,' he laughed. 'I don't believe all that stuff you learn at Sunday School. My Dad says the Bible is out of date. He says that no one who knows anything about science believes the Bible.'

Paul was just about to reply when the bell rang loudly for the end of school.

Paul and Sarah rushed home as fast as they could. They did, however, stop a few minutes to watch bricklayers building some apartments near their home. It was so interesting. Bricks and iron girders were everywhere, yet every man on the site seemed to know just what to do, and where everything went.

When at last they did arrive home, they burst through the front door, full of excitement.

'Look, Mum!' Sarah shouted as she undid her schoolbag to get out some of her new school books. 'We're going to have to work much harder this year at school.'

'We had to write today about what we liked most in the holidays.'

'What did you write about?' asked Mrs MacDonald.

'About our birthday party,' answered Paul.

'I wrote about all the presents we had,' added Sarah, 'and how we both got Bibles from our Sunday School teachers'

'We've brought home our new history text-books to cover, Mum,' explained Paul. 'Do you think Dad would mind our using some of that special paper he used to cover the book you gave him for his birthday?'

'That's a good idea,' agreed Mrs MacDonald. 'He won't mind at all, and there's plenty of it. Why don't you cover your new Bibles at the same time?'

'I hadn't thought of that,' said Paul.

'A good idea,' added Sarah.

'I'm glad you've both been given a new Bible,' answered Mrs MacDonald. 'Did you know that when Queen Elizabeth was crowned, she was presented with a Bible? She was given it because the Bible's the most important book in the world.'

'Why is it?' Paul and Sarah asked almost together.

'That's rather a large question to answer when I'm getting dinner ready! But the answer is because it's God's Book. Although lots of different men - probably as many as forty - wrote it, God made them want to write and helped them so that all they wrote is true.'

Sarah, like Paul, was always full of questions. 'Did those men know they were writing down God's words which would eventually be put together in one big book?'

'We don't know the answer to that,' replied Mrs MacDonald. 'Probably most of them knew that God was making them speak and write something special. I don't think though they would have guessed that their writings would be made one day into one book like the Bible. That makes it rather wonderful. God had a perfect plan from the beginning for all they wrote, although they didn't know it.'

'Philip looked over my shoulder and when he saw I was writing about my birthday presents and my new Bible, he laughed at me,' Paul said.

'Why did he do that?' asked Mrs MacDonald.

'He said something about the Bible being out of date, and that no one who knows science believes it,' Paul replied. 'I knew he wasn't right. But I didn't have a chance to reply because the bell rang for the end of school.'

Mrs MacDonald looked rather sad. 'I'm afraid there are lots of people who think and talk like Philip, Paul. They are out of date, and not the Bible. Lots of scientists believe the Bible is true. Mr Jones, the principal science teacher at the high school you will attend later, is a well-qualified scientist. He believes the Bible is true and reads it every day. Do you know what archaeologists and geologists are?'

Sarah answered right away. 'I saw a film on television about archaeologists. They dig up things from the earth and tell you from the pots and other things they find how people lived thousands of years ago.'

'A geologist studies stones and rocks,' added Paul, 'and can tell you how old the earth is.'

'You've the right idea,' replied Mrs MacDonald. 'Lots of things archaeologists and geologists have found out show that the history and the order of creation given in the Bible are true. So don't go thinking that science and the Bible won't go together! But I believe the Bible is true for lots of other good reasons.'

'Tell us some of them, please,' urged Sarah.

'Oh dear,' said Mrs MacDonald, looking at the clock, 'just look at the time! Dad will soon be home and I haven't finished getting his dinner ready. You'd better finish covering your books, and after dinner you can ask Dad why he believes the Bible is true.'

'All right,' replied Paul and Sarah. 'We know where all the things are.'

3 The Best Book

Paul and Sarah had decided how they were going to cover their history books and Bibles. They had seen their father cover his book a few weeks before. He had bought some attractive wrapping paper, printed to look like real leather. To strengthen the wrapping paper he had put strong brown paper underneath it. Then he had covered the wrapping paper with transparent plastic, which was sticky on one side. By turning the plastic over the edges of the wrapping paper, all three layers were firmly held together. Then he had fixed the new jacket to the top and bottom of the book with a strip of tape, inside the stiff covers.

The twins knew there had been quite a lot of wrapping paper left and that it had been put in the bottom of the kitchen cupboard with the brown paper. They were sure their father wouldn't mind them using it, especially as it was for covering their school books and their Bibles.

It was great fun copying what their father had done, although they made quite a mess. There were bits of paper everywhere - on the

table and on the floor as well!

When Mrs MacDonald came in to ask Sarah to set the table for dinner she was horrified to see the mess. 'You two rascals!' she shouted. 'Look at all these pieces of paper! I've a bone to pick with you. You're so untidy. Clear it up at once, or up to bed you go.'

'We'll do it right away,' Sarah promised.

****

Paul and Sarah's father had hardly settled down in his armchair after dinner before they showed him the new Bibles and the history books with their smart covers.

'Look what we've been doing!' said Paul.

Mr MacDonald looked at the covers. 'Where did you get that wrapping paper? I know what's happened. Someone has raided the cupboard in the kitchen. I'll take the price of that paper from your pocket money!'

He said this, pretending to be cross, but he couldn't keep from smiling, especially when he saw how worried the twins looked.

'Mum said we could use it and you wouldn't mind,' explained Paul, not sure whether his father was teasing or not.

Sarah thought she would change the subject quickly. 'She said you would tell us why you are sure the Bible is true, Dad.'

'Did she indeed!' he said. 'Well, I'll do my best. I'm sure there are lots of reasons I can give you. Let's begin with the age of the Bible. The Bible is the oldest book we have and it goes back further than any history book.'

Paul interrupted, 'When we got our new history books at school today, Dad, Mrs Fox said we were very fortunate to have them. Some of the books last year's class used were quite old, and even a bit out of date. Our new books have just been printed. We have a marvellous geography book too with lots of maps and photographs.'

'Yes,' replied Mr MacDonald. 'New books are always being written. Some of the science textbooks I had to read when I was at school would be no use to you because scientists know so much more now that the old books are out of date. But the Bible's never out of date. It's studied and read as much as ever. More copies of the Bible are sold every day in the world than most other books! '

'I didn't know that,' said Paul.

'Don't forget too,' continued Mr MacDonald, 'that it's amazing you have the Bible at all, at Sunday school or anywhere else. Often men have tried to destroy it. They've burned all the copies they could find, but they've never been able to get rid of it. Because the Bible is God's Book, He's kept it safe. In fact, there are more copies in the world now than ever before.'

Sarah said, 'I didn't know until Mum told us this afternoon that about forty men helped to write the Bible.'

'The amazing thing about that, Sarah, is that they all agree as much as they do. They didn't all write at the same time. The Bible took about a thousand years to write, and the writers didn't all speak the same language. They came from different countries. And yet the stories and writings fit together into one book. God had a plan for the Bible, just as an architect has a plan for a house, to help the builders put everything in its right place.'

'I hadn't thought of that,' said Sarah. 'We watched the builders across the street as we came home from school this afternoon. It seemed so confusing. I couldn't help wondering how they knew where to put everything.'

Mr MacDonald smiled, knowing what she meant.

Paul suddenly though't of something he had heard his father say before. 'Dad,' he said, 'you believe, don't you, that the Bible is true as well because so many things it says would happen have happened?'

'You have a good memory,' answered Mr MacDonald. 'No one would have thought in the early part of the twentieth century that the Jews would return to Palestine and be a nation called Israel; but the Bible, hundreds of years ago, said this would happen. You know, of course, that the Old Testament was written a long time before the New Testament. Some of God's messengers in the Old Testament - the prophets as they were called - had a lot to say about the Lord Jesus even before He was born at Bethlehem.'

'What did they say?' asked Paul.

'They said where He would be born, what would happen during His life, and most important of all how He would die and come to life again. Everything they said came exactly true. It was only because God told them these things that they knew what was going to happen. We don't know what is going to happen next year, quite apart from hundreds of years from now.'

Sarah remembered something. 'At Sunday School,' she said, 'we heard how missionaries spend time putting the Bible into other people's languages so they can read it themselves.'

'There's a very important reason for that,' answered Mr MacDonald, 'and it explains again why I'm sure the Bible is true. The Bible is able to change people's lives more than any other book in the world. It can change the unhappy lives of the fiercest tribe of South American Indians, and it can make a bad boy or girl good.'

'How can it do that?' asked Paul. 'I'm always getting into trouble! Either I make a mess, or I leave my room untidy. I keep making promises to do better, but I can never keep them.'

'I think you know the answer to that question, really, Paul,' replied Mr MacDonald. 'The Bible can make our lives better because it tells us how to become God's children through believing that the Lord Jesus died for our sins on the cross. And if we believe this message, it can teach us how to please God in our lives.'

Paul looked thoughtful. 'I hope I'll be able to tell Philip some of these things.'

4   Philip's questions

Paul and Sarah walked home from school the next day with Philip. Paul told Philip how they had covered their new Bibles as well as their history text-books, and he began to tell him some of the things his father had explained about the Bible.

'My Dad says that people who believe the Bible don't know what's happening around them,' jeered Philip.

'The Bible's a wonderful book,' replied Paul. 'It tells us the answer to lots of questions which can't be found anywhere else.'

'All right then,' said Philip, 'tell me the answer to some of my questions. Where did the first black people come from?'

'I don't know the answer to that,' Sarah whispered to Paul.

'Nor do I,' admitted Paul taken aback.

Philip asked some more questions and Sarah and Paul couldn't answer these either.

'There you are,' said Philip, 'the Bible doesn't tell you the answers to any questions!'

At this Philip pulled Paul's schoolbag and threw it on the pavement.

Paul tried to get even by grabbing Philip's schoolbag. Philip snatched at Paul's jacket and caught hold of Paul's right-hand pocket. When Paul tried to get away, he heard a dreadful tearing sound.

'Look what you've done, Philip! You've torn my jacket. I'll get into big trouble now.'

But Philip ran on ahead.

'Mum won't like it,' Sarah commented.

'You don't have to tell me that,' muttered Paul with a groan.

****

When the twins arrived home, Paul knew he had better tell his mother right away about the jacket. She would be bound to see it before long.

'Look what happened to my jacket on the way home,' he explained in a sorrowful voice. 'Philip did it. It was all his fault!'

'I'm sure you must have done something to Philip to make him do this to you. Were you taking something of his?' Mrs Mac-Donald asked.

'No,' answered Paul.

'Well, you were really,' interrupted Sarah.

'But he took my schoolbag,' said Paul, sticking up for himself. 'Then I grabbed his schoolbag; that was how it all started.'

Mrs MacDonald was really quite cross now. 'Never fight in the street,' she said. 'I know it's fun having a tussle now and again, but it's silly doing so in the street. A car might come along and knock you down. I'm not so cross about your torn pocket because I can repair that, but I don't want you ever fighting again or playing about in the street. Do you understand?'

Paul could see how serious and cross his mother was and he knew she was right. 'Yes,' said Paul.

'Why don't you both sit down for a moment and cool down? One of your favourite television programmes will be on soon.'

****

By the time the twins' father arrived home Paul had cooled down, and his mother had promised not to mention the jacket to his father if he promised not to play in the street again.

Paul and Sarah wanted to tell their father about Philip's questions.

'Dad, we told Philip why we believe the Bible is true,' said Sarah.

'Yes,' added Paul, 'and I think he was rather surprised that there are so many good reasons for believing the Bible, although he didn't say so.'

'And he asked us some very difficult questions we couldn't answer, Dad,' continued Sarah.

'What were they?' asked Mr MacDonald.

'Well, first of all, he wanted to know where the first black people came from, if we all came from Adam and Eve,' replied Sarah.

'We don't know what colour Adam and Eve were!' interrupted Mr MacDonald.

Paul added, 'He also asked us what language Adam and Eve spoke - and that was difficult! And then he asked how the Lord Jesus could have been with God when God made the world, when He hadn't even been born.'

Mr MacDonald smiled. 'Philip did ask you difficult questions, didn't he? Why did he ask these questions?'

Paul replied, 'Because he said that if the

Bible is really God's Book it will tell us the answers.'

'Let me ask you a question then,' said Mr MacDonald. 'If you wanted to learn something about history, would you go to your geography book?'

'Of course not, Dad,' Paul replied. 'We would get out our new history books and read them.'

'But wouldn't your geography books have some history in them somewhere?'

'Oh, yes,' Paul answered, 'but you wouldn't expect a geography book to have much history in it. A history book would be full of history. Anyone who went to a geography book to learn history might learn a little. But it would be silly to learn history like that!'

'Yes, of course,' said Mr MacDonald, 'but you see this is the mistake Philip is making. He's asking you a question which the Bible isn't written to answer. The Bible is written to show us the truth about God and to tell us how we can become His children. Of course, it tells how God made man. God made man perfect and made the colour of his skin just right for the part of the world he lived in. But the Bible isn't written to answer questions like that.'

'But the Bible does tell us things we can't find anywhere else about the first men and women, doesn't it, Dad?' asked Sarah.

'Yes, it does,' continued Mr MacDonald, 'but that's not its main purpose. Philip asked you about the language Adam and Eve spoke; the Bible does tell us something about this. It tells us that the whole earth spoke one language. Some people think that the first language was Hebrew - the language in which the Old Testament was written - but we don't know the answer to that really.'

Paul had been thinking about something as his father was speaking. 'The Bible will have a lot to say about Philip's question about the Lord Jesus, won't it?'

'Why do you say that?' Sarah asked Paul.

'Well, because the Bible is all about the Lord Jesus and was written to tell us the truth about God.'

'You're quite right,' said Mr MacDonald. 'Because the Bible isn't a history book, it won't answer all our questions about man, but because it's God's Book it will answer our questions about God. Now what was Philip's question?'

'How could Jesus have been with God when God made the world, when He hadn't even been born?' replied Paul.

'Do you know the answer to that, Sarah?' asked Mr MacDonald.

Sarah thought for a moment, and then said, 'Philip doesn't understand that Jesus is God and always has been God.'

'Quite right,' said Mr MacDonald. 'The Lord Jesus is God. He's the Son of God the Father. Because He's God He has no beginning and no end. That's hard for us to understand. There was a day when you were born and there has to be a day when you die.'

'Oh, Dad,' interrupted Sarah, 'at school today we heard about Florence Nightingale, the famous nurse. Mrs Fox wrote on the board "Florence Nightingale, Born 1820, Died 1910". She told us to write it in our books and to try to remember the dates. Then she asked who could tell her how long Florence Nightingale had lived.'

'Yes,' said Mr MacDonald, 'what was true

of Florence Nightingale will be true of all of us. There's a year when we're born and there will be a year when we die. But the Lord Jesus, being God, lives forever. He was with God the Father when the world was created and He was with Him before the world was created, too. If we were to be saved from our sins, someone who was a man, a perfect man, had to die for us in our place, taking the punishment for our sins. But there was no man good enough to do this. So the Lord Jesus, the Son of God, became a man so that He could die for us.'

Paul thought he understood now and so he said, 'Then that means that when Jesus was born in the stable at Bethlehem it wasn't the beginning of His life.'

'It certainly shows how much the Lord Jesus Christ loves us,' added Sarah. 'No wonder the Bible wants to tell us so much about Him. I wish you would tell us what God is like, Dad. How can He be three persons?'

'Hold on there. Those answers need plenty of time. It's too late tonight. Perhaps at the weekend we'll have more time to talk. That is if you go up to bed at once.'

5   Saturday morning

Saturday morning was always special in Paul and Sarah MacDonald's home because they didn't have to go to school.

And because Mr MacDonald didn't have to go to work on Saturdays, Mr and Mrs MacDonald were able to stay in bed just a little longer. They had said that now the twins were in Mrs Fox's class, they were old enough to make their parents a cup of morning coffee.

The twins were pleased about this. They were given careful instructions because Mrs MacDonald was afraid they might burn themselves. They would take turns doing it - one Saturday Paul would do it, and the next time would be Sarah's turn. They enjoyed getting up before their parents, especially as on a Saturday their comic came with the morning paper. The one who was not making coffee would be able to read it first.

'Who's going to make the coffee first?' asked Paul as they went downstairs to the kitchen.

'Look, there's a coin on the hall-table.

Let's toss for it,' suggested Sarah. 'Heads - you; tails - me.'

'All right,' agreed Paul, as he tossed the coin. 'Tails! Your turn, Sarah.'

Paul opened the front door and brought in the newspaper with the comic folded inside. He sat down and began to read it, while Sarah looked after the coffee. When it was ready, Sarah said, 'Well, I've made the coffee. You can take it up.'

'Oh, no,' said Paul, his head in the comic. 'Whoever makes it takes it up as well.'

'Now look,' argued Sarah,' you take it. And then I can look at the comic too.'

They started to quarrel. Mrs MacDonald heard them and shouted down the stairs, 'Say, you two! What's going on?'

'It's Paul!' cried Sarah.

'No, it isn't, you old tell-tale,' shouted Paul.

'Stop that kind of talk at once,' said Mrs MacDonald. 'If you can't make a cup of coffee without arguing, I'd better come down and make it myself.'

'All right,' said Paul, looking crossly at his sister. 'I'm coming.'

'Bring up the newspaper too, please,' Mr MacDonald called down.

****

By breakfast time Paul and Sarah were good friends again. Saturday was not a day to be spoiled by arguments. Their father would be home all day and sometimes they went out in the afternoon in the car.

On Saturday mornings there was more time than usual to read the Bible as a family. After breakfast, before washing the dishes, they got their Bibles and read a passage together. If Paul and Sarah didn't understand something, Mr and Mrs MacDonald would try to explain things to them.

This Saturday, they were reading John's Gospel, chapter four, when they came to verse twenty-four which says, 'God is spirit, and His worshippers must worship in spirit and in truth'.

When they came to the end of the passage Mr MacDonald asked, 'Any questions?'

'Yes, Dad, 'answered Paul. 'What does it mean when it says that God is spirit? What is God like? He must be very different from us, although I suppose we must be like Him in some ways.'

'Yes, you're right,' nodded Mr MacDonald. 'When we think of a person, we think of what he looks like. God is a person, but He has no body. That explains why He can be everywhere at once. Always remember that God is spirit, but that doesn't keep Him from being a real person.'

'It's rather hard to think of a person without a body!' said Sarah.

Her father smiled and said, 'Yes, it is to us because we've never lived without a body. Perhaps the best picture of God as spirit is your soul - it's the part of you which thinks and feels. You can't see your soul: and you can't see God. You can't touch your soul; and you can't touch God.'

'It's strange not being able to see your soul,' interrupted Sarah.

'Yes, but even so,' continued Mr MacDonald, 'you know it exists because it's the real you. Although we can't see God, we know He exists, and we know what He's like. If I said to you, Paul, "What's your friend Philip like?" I don't imagine that you would just say, "He's four feet nine inches tall with brown hair", but you would want to say things like, "He's my friend, he always asks a lot of questions, and we have a fight sometimes!"'

Paul looked a little ashamed, and wondered if his father knew about his jacket. But then he knew his mother kept her promises.

Mr MacDonald went on. 'In other words, more important than what Philip looks like, is the kind of person he is. That's what the Bible does. It doesn't tell me what God looks like. But it does tell me the kind of things God does and says.'

'Tell us some of the things the Bible says about God, please,' asked Sarah.

'Let Mum start,' replied Mr MacDonald.

Mrs MacDonald enjoyed helping the twins to understand. She thought for a moment and said, 'First of all, God is eternal: He has no beginning and no end. Everything - like the clothes we wear, for example - has a beginning and an end. God always has been and always will be.'

'Now you tell us something, Dad,' asked Paul.

'God is infinite,' Mr MacDonald replied. 'I'll try to explain what we mean by that. We are what we call "finite". There are lots of things we can't understand or do. We have to study to learn; and there's a limit to what we can know. But God knows everything. We can do many wonderful things, but sometimes a thing is too big for us. Nothing is too big for God. There's no end to His power. God is always greater than we can understand: that is what we mean when we say that God is infinite.'

'Can you spell infinite, Paul?' asked Mrs MacDonald.

'I think so - i-n-f-i-n-i-t-e,' Paul spelled out slowly.

'Your turn to tell us something more,' Sarah said to her mother.

'Well,' Mrs MacDonald replied, 'something the Bible often tells us about God is that He's holy. He's without any sin. God has never thought anything wrong, or said anything wrong, or done anything wrong. He's so pure that He can't even look at sin. When we see something unpleasant or wrong, we find it very easy to be inquisitive and want to look at it. God is so holy that He does not even want to look at it. He can never like things that are wrong.'

Before Paul and Sarah had time to ask any more questions, Mr MacDonald clapped his hands and said, 'That's all for now - we must help Mum clear up. Then if you two youngsters help me clean the car, we'll go for a drive this afternoon and we can continue talking then.'

'May I wash the car, Dad?' asked Paul.

'No, I want to do that!' shouted Sarah. 'Paul washed it last time.'

Before you could say 'Jack Robinson' Paul and Sarah were having another squabble over who was going to do what.

'I'll work it out,' decided Mr MacDonald. 'Sarah, you clean the windows. Paul, you do the bumpers, the lights and the wheels.'

'I'd rather not,' said Paul. 'I'd like to do the windows.'

'Listen here, young man,' said his father, 'you'll do that or nothing at all! I'll wash the body of the car and then there will be no more arguments. Perhaps Mum will vacuum inside for us. You can help her with that too, Paul.'

Half an hour later, when their work was complete, they all looked forward to their afternoon drive.

6 Out in the country

'Where are we going this afternoon for our drive?' Sarah asked her father.

'You can choose, if you like,' replied Mr MacDonald. 'We can go to the park, or we could go for a ride into the country, or to a forest and follow a nature trail.'

'Let's go to a forest,' cried Paul with excitement, 'and find a trail in the woods there!'

So as soon as they had had an early lunch they set off. It was fun going out in the car. If they were excited about getting somewhere their father always thought of games the twins could play as they went along. This made the time go more quickly.

They started off playing some of their own games first. 'Let's play "I spy",' suggested Sarah. So for about ten minutes they played "I spy", but they soon got tired of it.

'Let's do something different,' suggested Mr MacDonald. 'It's to do with the names of the places we may see on our journey, and it takes a long time. We have to find the names of places according to the letters of the alphabet.'

'Which ones?' interrupted Sarah, looking puzzled.

'From the beginning of the alphabet, silly!' exclaimed Paul. 'Girls don't always use their heads!'

'Now, now,' interrupted Mr MacDonald. 'We look for the name of a place beginning with the letter A. Then we begin to look for one with the letter B, and so on. We'll see how far we can get.'

'It's going to be hard to find one with the letter Z,' Sarah said.

Mr MacDonald smiled. 'We'll face that problem when we get to it,' he replied.

'It will take ages,' gasped Paul.

'That will make it all the more fun,' laughed Mr MacDonald. 'Whenever we go out together in the car we can continue playing this game, even when we're playing others.'

'There's the name of a town beginning with C,' shouted Paul, looking at a road sign.

'That's no good.'

'There's also one beginning with G,' added Sarah.

'No good either,' replied their father.

It did not seem long before they reached

the forest and they had already found the names of places beginning with A, B, C and D.

'Perhaps we'll see an E if we go a different route home,' suggested Mrs MacDonald, seeing the twins were a little disappointed. 'So remember to keep your eyes open.'

Paul and Sarah were thrilled at being in the country. In school they were learning a lot about nature, so they wanted to look at as many different plants, trees and leaves as they could.

Suddenly Sarah noticed a sign on a path showing the way to a beauty spot at a place called Erie. 'Look!' she shouted. 'I've found one.'

'Found what?' asked Paul.

'A place beginning with the letter E,' said Sarah triumphantly.

After a while Paul and Sarah had seen enough to satisfy them and they were hungry too.

Paul sat down on the grass with a sigh. 'What is there to eat, Mum?'

'Egg salad sandwiches, tomato sandwiches, peanut-butter sandwiches, potato chips and

cake,' answered Mrs MacDonald.

'Oooh, stop!' cried Sarah. 'I feel like old Mole in The Wind in the Willows when Ratty told him what they had for their picnic - I'm so hungry.'

'Let's stop talking and begin eating,' suggested Paul.

'Which grace shall we pray?' asked Mrs MacDonald.

'"Praise God from whom all blessings flow" would be a good one out in the country, wouldn't it?' suggested Mr MacDonald. 'Why don't we sing it together?'

When they had finished the sandwiches, Paul was ready to talk again.

'Look at the lovely lines on that leaf I found, Dad,' he said.

'It's wonderful to think that God made all the things we've seen and collected this afternoon, isn't it?' added Sarah.

'Yes,' agreed Mr MacDonald, 'absolutely everything, and He made them all perfect, like the veins on Paul's leaf.'

'Is there only one God?' Paul asked, thinking of a question he had asked his father the other day.

'Yes,' said Mrs MacDonald.

'Is Jesus God too?' Paul then asked.

Again his mother said, 'Yes.'

'Is the Holy Spirit God as well?' asked Paul.

Sarah understood now what Paul was thinking, so she asked her father, 'How can there be only one God, then? Surely there are three Gods - the Father, Jesus and the Holy Spirit?'

Mr MacDonald smiled. 'No, there's only one God. He's the God who made the world and the God who has given us the Bible. He makes Himself known to us in three different Persons we call the Trinity.'

'What does Trinity mean?' asked Sarah, for she liked finding out the meaning of new words.

'"Trinity" comes from two words: tri - meaning three - and unity - meaning one. The Bible speaks of three Persons - the Father, the Son and the Holy Spirit - but tells us they are one.'

'I don't understand how three things can be one,' exclaimed Paul.

'Let me try and help you understand,' replied his mother. 'Pick me one of those clover leaves, please. Now, how many parts are there to it?'

Paul put the remains of his doughnut into his mouth before he reached for a clover leaf.

'Three parts,' answered Paul.

'But how many leaves are there?' Mrs MacDonald asked.

'One,' answered Paul.

'Look,' said Paul's father, as he drew a triangle on the ground with a stick. 'How many sides has this triangle?'

'Three,' answered Paul and Sarah together.

'All right then, how many triangles do they make?' he asked.

'One, of course!' they answered.

'How many of us are there here?' asked Mrs MacDonald.

'Why, four,' said Sarah.

'How many families are here then?' asked her mother next.

'Only one,' Paul and Sarah replied.

'Perhaps now you can see,' explained Mr MacDonald, 'that there are many different kinds of oneness. Although God makes

Himself known to us as three Persons, He also tells us that He is one, and that there is only one God.'

'It isn't easy to understand, though, is it?' Paul said thoughtfully. 'I wouldn't find it easy to explain to someone like Philip.'

'No, you're right,' agreed Mr MacDonald, 'but remember we're talking about God who is very great and our minds are much too small to understand everything about Him.'

Sarah had a question. 'Did the disciples understand it, do you think?' She knew the disciples were just ordinary people.

'I'm sure they didn't understand it completely, Sarah,' answered her father, 'but I know that they believed it. They were Jews and they knew there's only one God, who made everything. But then they met the Lord Jesus and they lived with Him for three years. As they lived with Him they came to realise that He was not only a man, but that He was also God. They were very surprised to discover this.'

'They must have been,' commented Paul. 'Imagine finding out that your friend was God!'

Mr MacDonald nodded and continued.

'Before the Lord Jesus left the disciples He promised to send Someone just like Himself to live inside them - the Holy Spirit. The disciples saw the Lord Jesus return to heaven. Not long after, at Pentecost, the Holy Spirit came to live within the disciples to give them power to be the Lord Jesus' messengers. They knew the Holy Spirit was God. But they knew He wasn't the Father. And they knew He wasn't the Lord Jesus, for He had returned to heaven. So although they couldn't fully understand it, they knew that God is a Trinity, three in one.'

Mrs MacDonald had thought of something else. 'When you get home this evening, you could read the story of the Lord Jesus' baptism in the Gospels. The Lord Jesus, the second Person of the Trinity, was being baptised. As He came out of the water, He saw the Holy Spirit, the third Person of the Trinity, coming down like a dove, to rest on Him.'

'I remember now,' said Sarah. 'Didn't God then say something about the Lord Jesus?'

'Yes,' replied Mrs MacDonald, 'at the same time, God the Father, the first Person of the Trinity, spoke from heaven, saying,

'You are My Son, whom I love; with You I am well pleased.' The Bible doesn't explain how God can be three yet one; but it simply tells us that this is the truth.'

Mr MacDonald looked at his watch. 'It's almost time we were on our way,' he said. 'Let's pack everything and put it in the car.'

When they had packed up, the twins had a quick look round the field they were in, for anything they had missed. They walked along the hedges but couldn't find any flowers or trees they hadn't seen already.

But there were lots of pieces of paper which had blown from people's picnics.

'Pick up the pieces of paper, please,' said Mr MacDonald.

'Do we need to?' asked Paul.

'Yes indeed,' replied his father. 'When you've put them in the litter basket, you look at what it says on the side.'

So they picked up all the paper they could see and took it to the basket. Attached there was a metal sign, which read, 'Please keep the forest preserve tidy'.

Not long after, they were on their way home in the car.

'The windows are dirty, Sarah,' said Paul.

'I would expect them to be, with your messy fingers on them all the time,' said Mrs MacDonald, defending Sarah who had worked hard on the car windows.

They sped along the highway back to their home.

'Look!' shouted Paul. 'There's a letter F!'

'That makes three points to you and two to me, then,' said Sarah, peering out of the window to see if she could see the name of a place beginning with the letter G.

7 An afternoon walk

On Sunday mornings Paul and Sarah went to
Sunday School at 9.30. That was why Mr and
Mrs MacDonald had their longer time in bed
on Saturday morning instead of on Sunday.
There were quite a few things to be done
before the twins went to Sunday School if
their mother was to get lunch ready quickly
after they all came home from church. Mr
and Mrs MacDonald always met Paul and
Sarah after Sunday School outside the church
so they could go into church together for the
service at eleven o'clock.

Paul and Sarah were in different classes
because there were boys' and girls' classes for
each age group. Sarah was in Miss Leonard's
class and Paul was in Mr Eaton's. But they
both had the same lesson. This Sunday it was
on something they had heard about several
times before. It was all about how God made
the world.

Sarah was especially glad because she
remembered only the previous afternoon she
had asked her father whether God had made
absolutely everything. She told Miss Leonard

this. She also told her about the trip she and Paul had had into the country, and how many different sorts of leaves they had collected to take to school on Monday.

****

It was a lovely day as Mr and Mrs MacDonald, Paul and Sarah walked home after church.

'Could we go out for a walk this afternoon?' Mrs MacDonald asked her husband.

'Would you like that?' he asked the twins.

'Oh, yes please, Dad,' said the twins in chorus.

When everything had been cleared away after lunch, Mr MacDonald said, 'We'll jump into the car and we'll drive up to the park. We'll walk to the gardens at the top of the hill, and then back again the short way.'

The twins particularly liked these gardens. Besides all the lawns and flowerbeds, there were some beautiful ponds, a well and a sundial to see and examine.

'What was your Sunday School lesson this morning?' Mrs MacDonald asked when they were walking through the park, after they had left the car.

'Oh, it was all about creation,' answered Sarah. 'We read how God made the world.'

'Good,' said Mr MacDonald. 'How about playing "True or False"? I'll say something about what I expect you heard this morning and you tell me whether it's true or false.'

'That's a good idea,' said Paul. 'Can either of us answer?'

'Yes,' replied Mr MacDonald. 'But take turns to give the answer first. Then if you think the other person is wrong, you can give the correct answer. All right?'

Paul and Sarah nodded.

'The world just happened - by accident,' stated Mr MacDonald. 'True or false? You start, Sarah.'

'False, Dad,' she answered.

'Yes, that's right.'

Paul had a question. 'But how can you be sure, Dad? Mr Eaton said there are some people who say it just happened; but that the Bible proves them wrong. But how can we be sure?'

'Don't you remember what you did yesterday?' asked Mr MacDonald, thinking of how Paul had looked so closely at the veins of the leaf he had picked. 'Look! Pick that dandelion in the grass.'

So Paul went and picked it.

'Just look at its stalk and its petals. How perfectly they're made! What a difference between that and some of the artificial flowers we have at home!'

'It's amazing, isn't it?' said Paul as he looked very closely.

'Now, if you picked up a wristwatch in the grass, Paul,' continued Mr MacDonald, 'would you say that it just happened?'

'Course not,' answered Paul. 'I should say someone had made it and that then someone else had bought it.'

'Well,' said Mr MacDonald, 'remember the dandelion you picked was far more wonderful than any wristwatch you might accidentally find in the grass. A wristwatch can go wrong and has no real life in it. But the dandelion has life in it and although you've picked it, its roots will grow another one in due course. Such a thing couldn't just have happened.' Paul was quite impressed by what his father said and saw the point.

The sun had attracted lots of people to the park besides the MacDonald family. Many of them were taking their dogs for a walk.

It wasn't long before they came to the gardens at the top of the hill. There were even more people there. But the gardens were very large, so there was room for everyone without being too squashed. The flower beds looked beautiful. There were great splashes of colour made by the clumps of flowers.

'God made the flowers after the birds,' said Mr MacDonald. 'True or false?'

'False,' declared Paul. 'He made the flowers before the birds.'

'You've a good memory,' commented his mother. 'I don't know that I would have remembered that. I would have had to look it up in the Bible, I think.'

'Your turn, Sarah,' said Mr MacDonald. 'The part of the Bible which tells us most about creation is Genesis, chapter one.'

'True,' answered Sarah.

'Look at that pond,' shouted Paul. The twins ran very quickly to it. Their parents caught up with them slowly. It was indeed a splendid pond, full of goldfish.

'Another question for you, twins,' suggested Mr MacDonald. 'God created the world in seven days.'

'False,' answered Paul.

'No, true,' shouted Sarah.

'No, you're wrong,' explained Mr MacDonald to Sarah. 'Paul is right. It was in six days that God made the world and He rested on the seventh day.'

'Oh, yes,' said Sarah with a frown.

'Look at those lovely rose beds,' exclaimed Mrs MacDonald. 'They're going to be wonderful when they flower. I wish we had pruned ours as carefully.'

Paul remembered something Philip had said once. 'Dad, what would you say to Philip if he said to you, "How can you prove that God made the world?" He says, "How can you be sure, when no one saw God do it?"'

Mr MacDonald smiled. He knew it wasn't an easy question to answer, and his answer wouldn't be easy to understand. 'You can't prove it if you mean proving it like proving two and two make four,' he said. 'But you see there are lots of clues all around us that confirm that God made the world.'

'What kind of clues?' Paul asked.

'Well, think of that dandelion you picked in the grass. If you see a painting, you know there must have been a painter or an artist. If you see a building, you know that a builder made it. If you see the latest model of a car, you know that someone designed it. Just look at those flower beds over there. Do you see how the plants are in perfect rows? Do you think that just happened?'

'Of course not,' answered Sarah. 'One of the gardeners must have laid it out very carefully.'

'In the same way,' explained Mr MacDonald, 'wherever we look in the world we see clues that everything that exists has thought and care behind it.'

'That's really what I said to Philip,' Paul said. 'I said to him, "If God didn't make the world, who did?"'

Mrs MacDonald laughed. 'That wasn't a bad answer.'

'Yes,' agreed Mr MacDonald, nodding his head, 'but most of all I'm sure that God made everything because of what the Bible says. We know lots of reasons why the Bible is true - we've talked about them, haven't we? The Bible tells us time and time again that God is the Creator. I know God created everything, not because I can prove it, but because I believe what God says.'

Sarah asked, 'Does the Bible tell us how God made the world? Sort of how He did it?'

'No, Sarah,' answered her father. 'The Bible doesn't tell us that. You must remember that the Bible doesn't set out to be a kind of encyclopedia on every subject! It sets out to tell us the truth about God and about ourselves. One of the first things it teaches us is that God is our Maker and all the good things we enjoy come from Him.'

'It will soon be time for us to go home,' Mrs MacDonald reminded them. 'Where would you like to spend your last few minutes?'

'May we go and have a look at the sundial?' asked Paul. 'I haven't been up here before when the sun's been shining. I'd like to see how the sundial works.'

It was fun trying to work out the time from the sundial. By the way the shadow was

cast by the sun, they could see without looking at Mr MacDonald's watch that it was getting late.

'One more question for you, twins,' suggested Mr MacDonald. 'God made the lesser light to rule the night and the greater light to rule the day. True or false?'

'True,' said Sarah.

It wasn't long before they were back in the car on their way home. Paul and Sarah felt they had had a good time.

'We've enjoyed this weekend,' said Sarah. 'Can we go out again next week-end?'

'It all depends how you behave this week,' replied Mrs MacDonald. But before she could say that she expected they could, Paul shouted, 'There's a letter G.'

And sure enough there was a sign to a place beginning with the letter G.

'I'd forgotten all about our game,' said Mr MacDonald. 'That's pretty good going, getting up to the letter G in one week-end. I wonder how much farther we'll get by this time next week.'

'I'll keep a good look-out next time we're out together,' said Sarah. 'Paul has noticed more than I have.'

'There's plenty of time for you to catch up, Sarah,' encouraged Mrs MacDonald. 'There are a lot more letters of the alphabet left!'

published by
Christian Focus Publications

THE LORD IS MY SHEPHERD

by
Lois Veals
illustrations
by
Janis Mennie

a book about Psalm 23 with pictures to colour

*Lois Veals has also written
two other books for children*
REJOICE AND BE GLAD
a book about the Beatitudes
OUR FATHER
a book about the Lord's Prayer

The Puzzling Book

compiled by
KIRSTI PATERSON
and illustrated by
JANIS MENNIE

The puzzles in this book are based on the New International Version of the Bible.

There are six sections, each containing up to eight puzzles.

An invaluable resource for Sunday School and day-school teachers, as well as teaching vital Bible truths to children in the 10-12 year old age group.

Other puzzle books published by Christian Focus Publications include:

CHRISTIAN ARMOUR
DANIEL AND HIS THREE FRIENDS
DAVID AND GOLIATH
MOSES
NOAH'S ARK
THE NAMES OF JESUS
PEOPLE JESUS MET

Helen
of the Glen

by

George Maclean

A story set in the times of the Covenanters that tells about the faith of a girl and her brother as they continue to worship God despite all the dangers that it involves.

published by

Christian Focus Publications